ENTRANCE TO THE CAVE (FROM THE INSIDE).

ONE HUNDRED MILES IN MAMMOTH CAVE —IN 1880

by H. C. Hovey

EDITOR'S PREFACE

What was a trip like a century ago to America's most popular cave? Author Hovey here tells of his trip at that time—an extended one that included much more than the already-developed tourist route. He narrates the cave's early history and gives insights on how it was formed, while describing the formations his party found and the explorations they made.

Cave buffs and casual visitors will appreciate this perspective of history in the first person. Enhancing the text are a number of period illustrations, several of which accompanied the original article in *Scribner's Monthly* for 1880, then a national magazine. Others have been added from similar contemporary sources, as *Century Magazine* (1898), *Scribner's Monthly* (1874), *Scribner's Magazine* (1887), and *Picturesque America* (1874).

Acknowledgements are due long-time cave explorer Don Bloch, now proprietor of the Collectors' Center antiquarian bookstore in Denver. He provided advice on the reprint, and furnished some of the original materials.

Our author hopes in his sketch that Mammoth Cave will be well cared for in the future and yet that public access may continue and even be improved. Now is that future he imagined, and we suspect that he may be satisfied with the result, for in 1941 the area was formally established as a national park. The idea was to preserve the area for use for all time.

Today Mammoth Cave is visited by millions of people every year and has been explored and mapped for nearly 200 miles, making it the longest recorded cave system in the world.

William R. Jones

THE ENTRANCE TO MAMMOTH CAVE (LOOKING OUT).

ISBN 0-89646-054-1

Sink holes, Edmonson County, Ky.

ONE HUNDRED MILES IN MAMMOTH CAVE.

by H. C. Hovey

THE cavernous limestone of Kentucky covers an area of 8000 square miles; and a ride of eighty-five miles on the Louisville and Great Southern Railroad took my companion and myself to the heart of this wonderful region.

We left the cars at Cave City—only a cluster of houses amid the cornfields—and mounted to the top seat of an old-fashioned stage-coach, that makes daily trips to Mammoth Cave, ten miles distant. Edmondson County, within whose limits it is located, has about 4000 sink-holes and 500 open caverns, many of which are but nameless grottoes, while others have gained celebrity. The road winds among the hills and across a high table-land to the bluffs of Green River. The soil is comparatively sterile, the farms are few and poorly tilled, and large tracts of woodland seem to be yet untouched by the ax. Openings are observed here and there amid the rocks, each being, as the driver assured us, the mouth of a cave.

"Are any of them," I asked, "equal to Mammoth Cave?"

"No, siree," responded Jehu, with a crack of the whip that made the leaders prance, "I reckon it's wuth fifty sich holes in the groun'. What's your notion about it, Jedge?"

"I have visited the chief caverns of the West," replied the judge, "and in my opinion, going from any one of them to Mammoth Cave is like exchanging a log cabin for a palace."

A medley of legends and anecdotes was then served up for us in Corn-cracker vernacular, with accounts of Diamond, Salts, White, Short, the Grand Crystal and Proctor's caves, and others of less note.

A bugle-flourish heralded our arrival at the Cave Hotel,—a spacious building evolved from a log-cabin germ,—and brought around the coach a throng of guests expecting friends, and negro servants offering to take our luggage.

The hotel register shows an aggregate of over 2000 visitors a year. Adjoining the office is a cabinet where specimens are for sale; the rules judiciously forbidding visitors to help themselves. Another rule prohibits the use of surveyors' instruments. lest some unscrupulous person should find a new entrance beyond the 2000 acres now comprising the estate, and steal the cave. Such maps as have been published are therefore not correct, having been prepared without accurate measurement.

The regular hour for entering the cave is nine A. M. The proprietor, Captain W. S. Miller, on learning our errand, generously gave us a special guide, and the freedom of the cave as long as we continued our explorations. An outfit includes a close-fitting cap, easy shoes, a stout dress, a walking-stick, a swinging lamp and some matches. The guide for each party carries extra lamps, a can of lard oil, a lunch basket and a haversack of fire-works. Thus equipped, each working-day for a fortnight beheld us following Tom Lee, our special guide, down

MAMMOTH CAVE—THE BOAT RIDE ON ECHO RIVER.

the shady path to the mouth of the cave. The other guides, colored men, are familiarly known as Old Mat, Old Nick, and William. The original guide, whose daring exploits and striking traits made him famous, was Stephen Bishop; his remains now rest in the tangled grave-yard near the garden.

Mammoth Cave has a noble vestibule! Amid tulip-trees and grape-vines, maples and butternuts, fringing ferns and green mosses, is the entrance to this under-ground palace. From a frowning ledge a cascade leaps to the rocks below, where it vanishes at once, forming no running stream. The former entrance, through which the discoverer, a hunter named Hutchins, in 1809, made his way in pursuit of a bear, is near the bank of Green River, about half a mile distant. Since that day the roof has fallen in, cutting off a section now known as Dixon's Cave, and leaving the present mouth; which is 194 feet above water level, and 118 feet below the summit of the bluff on which stands the hotel.

A winding flight of seventy stone steps conducts us around the cascade, into an antechamber. At the end of this is a grated iron door to which each guide has a key. The cave, originally bought for forty dollars, is now valued at $250,000; and this formidable door protects it from spoliation.

As we cross the portal, a strong current

STEPHEN BISHOP, THE GUIDE.

ENTRANCE (WINTER).

of air blows out our lights, but a few yards within, where the draft is weaker, we re-kindle them. This phenomenon, which I had previously observed in Wyandot and other large caves, is due to a marked difference in temperature between the atmosphere within, and that without the cave. Both the air and the water in the cave nearly correspond with the heat of the earth itself, which in that latitude varies but little from 56° Fahrenheit throughout the year. In some of the dryer chambers the mercury rises to 58°, and in some of the springs and pools it falls to 52°. On our first visit, the thermometer at the hotel office indicated 100° in the shade, a difference on that day of more than 40°, which caused, of course, a strong outward flow. The current is said to set inward in cold weather, when the conditions are reversed. Chemical processes also are continually at work, surcharging the cave atmosphere with oxygen, and of course forcing it out as the volume expands. I was informed that Salts Cave, not far distant, in which these chemical agencies are much more active, never inhales at all, but exhales all the year round.

The first objects exhibited to visitors are the relics of saltpeter works in the Rotunda. Ruts of cart-wheels and hoof-prints of oxen remain in the indurated clay, leading to the pumps, pipes, and eight large vats, from which, during the war of 1812, Mr. Archibald Miller took niter to Philadelphia by wagon, to be used in making gunpowder. Log benches are still exhibited where once sat swarthy miners, before a rocky pulpit, to hear of Him to whom the darkness and the light are both alike.

In 1816, the property passed into the hands of a Mr. Moore, who was ruined by complicity with Burr and Blennerhasset. It was successively owned by Gatewood, Gorin, and Dr. Croghan, to whose heirs it still belongs.

The simple truth about Mammoth Cave surpasses the most ingeniously woven fabrication. Its areal diameter is nine or ten miles. Its known and numbered avenues are 223, and their united length equals from 150 to 200 miles. Twelve million cubic yards of space have here been excavated from the rocks by the agency of air and of water.* Such are the windings, crossings and involutions of this labyrinth, that we found, by the time our explorations were ended, on adding up all our daily trips in and out, we had traveled about one hundred miles under-ground!

The Main Cave, so called in distinction from minor avenues opening into it, extends like a deserted river-bed, through a succession of noble arches and domes, to a point six miles within, where it is abruptly closed by fallen rocks.

New objects of interest met us at every step, as we advanced. During a moment's pause we were startled by what seemed the loud ticking of a musical time-piece. It was but the measured melody of water dripping into a basin hidden behind the rocks. Drop

* There is a well-known tendency to overstate the marvelous, and several writers of repute insist on far lower figures than are given here. The above estimates, however, agree with the Kentucky Geological reports of Owen (1856-1861), and are confirmed by the new survey now being made, under the direction of Professor N. S. Shaler.

THE GIANT'S COFFIN, MAMMOTH CAVE.

MAMMOTH CAVE—THE SUBTERRANEAN ALBUM.

by drop monotonously it falls, as it has fallen, it may be, for a thousand years.

Not far from this natural water-clock, is a symmetrical recess chiseled by a tiny rill, whose limpid water is collected in a little pool. The story is told of a poor blind boy, who rambled over the country winning a precarious living by his violin, and who, as he said, was resolved to *see* the cave for himself. He lost his way, and when found by his companions was quietly sleeping beside this basin, which ever since has been called " Wandering Willie's Spring."

Singular effects are produced for a long distance beyond this point by the incrustations of gypsum stained by the black oxide of iron, seeming to cut gigantic silhouettes from the ceiling of white limestone. At first we ridiculed these fancies, but at last they fascinated us. Bears, monkeys, ant-eaters, catamounts,—indeed, a whole menagerie is on exhibition, including the old mammoth himself. We were especially interested in a side-show of a giant and giantess playfully tossing papooses to and fro. The Giant's Coffin is near by—a rock shaped like a mighty sarcophagus. It is detached from the ceiling, walls and floor, resting its weight on stone trestles, and equals in size one of the famous blocks of Baalbek, being forty feet long, twenty wide and eight deep.

Here the trend of the Main Cave turns upon itself at an acute angle. The apex of the angle is marked by McPherson's monument, a rude pile of stones in memory of a gallant soldier. More than three hundred such monuments have been erected in different portions of the cave, in honor of various individuals, literary institutions and the several States of the Union. Some of these pillars reach from floor to roof, each tourist who chooses to do so adding a stone. An incidental benefit of this custom is that it has helped to clear the paths.

The rules strictly forbid any defacement of the walls. Candles were formerly a favorite means of smirching the names of visitors, in lamp-black, on the plaster-like ceiling, where it was low enough to be within reach. This is now especially interdicted; and instead of these rocky albums there are receptacles for visiting and business cards, thousands of which are thus accumulated, representing visitors from all parts of the world.

The roofless remains of two stone cottages are next visited, as having a melancholy history. These, and some frame ones, now torn down, were built in 1843 for fifteen consumptive patients, who here took up their abode, induced to do so by the uniformity of temperature and highly oxygenated air, which possesses the purity without the rarity of the air at high altitudes. The experiment was an utter failure.

A strangely beautiful transformation scene is exhibited in the Star Chamber, a hall seventy feet wide, sixty high and five hundred long. The lofty ceiling is coated with black gypsum, studded with thousands of white spots, caused by the efflorescence of the sulphate of magnesia. Our guide asks us to sit down on a log bench by the wall, and then, collecting the lamps, vanishes behind

THE STAR CHAMBER.

a jutting rock; whence, by adroit manipulations, he throws shadows flitting like clouds athwart the starry vault. The effect is extremely fine, and the illusion is complete. One can easily persuade himself that the roof is removed, and that he looks up from a deep valley into the real heavens.

"Good-night," says Tom; "I will see you again in the morning."

With this abrupt leave-taking he plunges into a gorge, and we are in utter darkness. Even the blackest midnight in the upper world has from some quarter a few scattered rays; but here the gloom is without a gleam. In the absolute silence that ensues, we hear the beating of our hearts. The painful suspense is at length broken by one of those strange outbursts of laughter that come when least expected; and then we indignantly ask each other the meaning of this sudden desertion. But while we are roundly berating the guide's treachery, we see in the remote distance a faint glimmer, like the first streak of dawn. The light increases in volume till it tinges the tips of the rocks, like tops of hills far away. The horizon is bathed in rosy hues, and we are prepared to see the sun rise, when all at once the guide appears, swinging his cluster of lamps, and asking us how we like the performance. Loudly encored, he repeats the transformations again and again,—starlight, moonlight, thunder-clouds, midnight and day-dawn, heralded by cock-crowing, the barking of dogs, lowing of cattle and various other farm-yard sounds; until, weary of an entertainment that long ago lost its novelty for him, he bids us resume our line of march.

As we pass along under a mottled ceiling that changes, from the constellation just described, to a mackerel sky with fleecy masses of floating clouds, many curious objects are pointed out to us. Here is a stout oak-pole, projecting from a crevice, now inaccessible—put there when, and by whom, and for what purpose? There are snow-drifts of native Epsom salts, whitening the dusky ledges. Spaces are shown completely covered by broad slabs, underneath which are the ashes and embers of ancient fires. Side-cuts occasionally tempt us from the beaten path, into which we return by a circuitous way. Crossing the solitary chambers, we enter the Fairy Grotto, whose alabaster grove of stalactites has been despoiled by ruthless hands. Skirting a pit, down whose abyss a cataract tumbles, we climb hills, plunge into gorges, walk underneath frowning cliffs, until we have explored the main cave from end to end.

No creeping nor crawling has to be done here. The average width of this immense natural tunnel is about sixty feet, and its height forty feet; but portions expand to much greater dimensions. Proctor's Arcade is said to be one hundred feet wide, fifty feet high, and a thousand yards long. By burning magnesium lights at several points at once, each light being equivalent to seventy candles, we surveyed the whole vista. In like manner we illuminated Wright's Rotunda, 400 feet in diameter. But the funereal darkness of the Black Chamber defied magnesium, and refused to be cheered even by red fire.

We lingered long amid the wonders of the Chief City, where several acres are strewn with rocks like ancient ruins, the whole area being overarched by so vast a dome as to make us wonder if it has an adequate key-stone.

"Why doesn't it fall?" inquired Barton.

"I know of no reason why it should not

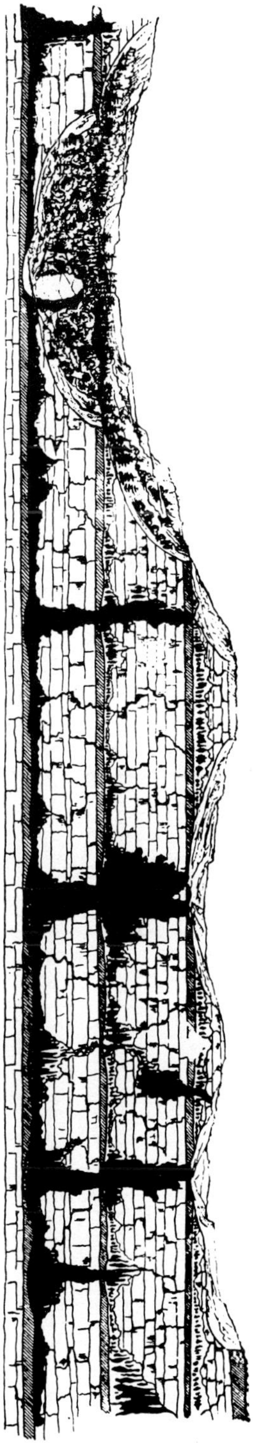

Showing the Formations of Caverns in Limestone. (In the distance a natural bridge, the remains of a great cavern.)

CHIEF CITY.

fall at this very moment," said Tom, solemnly, "and I never come underneath without some degree of fear. Yet the arch appears to be a solid block of seamless limestone, and it may stand for a thousand years. You can see, from these Indian torches, that the place is now precisely what it has been for centuries."

As he spoke, the guide picked up some half-burnt bits of cane, which, as he assured us, the red men used to fill with bear's fat and burn, to light them on their search for flint mines, alabaster quarries and other coveted treasures. Igniting our fire-works, we threw a glare over the long slope of irregular rocks, and athwart the gigantic vault, bringing such glories to view as no torch-bearing mound-builder ever saw. And while the crimson light died away amid the arches and pinnacles, we took leave, with many a backward look, of this prehistoric council-hall of sagamores and dusky braves.*

The proprietors object to anything that will mar the romantic rudeness of this ancient cavern. Yet a little of it might well be sacrificed to the spirit of modern invention. Electric lights would grandly illuminate the large halls and domes. Telephones would be of advantage, in establishing communication with the outer world. Tramways might be laid through the main cave and the more accessible avenues. Shafts might be opened at certain terminal points, known to be near the surface, through which visitors might be taken up by elevators, and conveyed back to the hotel in hacks, instead of wearily retracing their steps, as must now be done. Increased patronage would soon cover the cost of such improvements; and time and strength would thus be saved for exploring portions of the cave whose picturesque scenery is now rarely beheld, except by the most resolute pedestrians.

It is doubtful if one visitor in fifty goes farther into the main cave than to the Star Chamber; but none fail to see this favorite hall of illusions. We revisited it frequently during our stay. The path to it is dry and well trodden. A pleasing incident comes to mind, showing how easily it may be reached, although more than a mile under-ground. One evening, after tea, I had entered thus far alone, without a guide, and after studying for a while the peculiar effects of light and shade, I sat down on the log bench and put my lamps out, in order to enjoy the luxury of utter darkness, silence and solitude. But ere long voices were heard, and mysterious peals of laughter. Soon the day-dawn effect was unexpectedly produced, by the approach of a party of jocund youths and maidens, with lights, who, having dressed for a hop, first paid a visit to this enchanted ground, and as cave dust never flies nor sticks, they did so without a speck on polished boots or trailing robes.

* Monographs have been published by the State Geological Survey, on the Cavern-dwelling Races, and Prehistoric Remains of Kentucky; and additional memoirs on the same subjects are promised.

Tourists are usually hurried through by two routes, one requiring four hours and the other nine, and both together covering about twenty-five miles of travel in and out. Our more leisurely exploration led us along many an unfrequented path, and allowed us to linger at will in the most interesting localities. The avenues, as all side-passages are termed, vary in importance, some of them rivaling the main cave, while others involve grievous climbing and crawling, with small recompense.

Audubon's Avenue lies nearest the entrance. It is chiefly noted for its myriads of bats, and for the fact that it leads to an opening into which a miner dropped his lamp in 1812. Matt, the guide, found it thirty years afterward at the bottom of Mammoth Dome, a place to be reached only by a long detour.

The Gothic Arcade is approached by a stair-way from galleries beyond the saltpeter vats. Here a niche is pointed out where the early explorers are said to have found two Indian mummies, a woman and a child, along with fine fabrics and trinkets, necklaces of deers' hoofs and eagles' claws, and all that could please the barbaric taste.*

The chapel in the Gothic Arcade has an arched roof supported by large stalagmitic columns, once beautiful but now sullied by sacrilegious smoke. I counted eight, and found fragments of about thirty more. Their growth was slow, requiring many centuries to develop their present dimensions. Three of the pillars are so grouped as to form two Gothic arches. Before this unique altar once stood a runaway bride, who had

* Forwood, in his excellent manual on Mammoth Cave (pp. 170-194), has collected all existing accounts of these extraordinary relics. Hon. F. Gorin, a former owner of the cave, disputes their authenticity. He states, however, that the skeleton of a giant, and that of an infant, were found in 1811 in Audubon's Avenue; and that mummies were found in Short Cave. Sandals, shreds of garments, etc., from Salts Cave, in the vicinity of Mammoth, are exhibited in the archæological museum of Harvard College, and have been lately described by Prof. F. W. Putnam.

MAMMOTH DOME.

promised her anxious mother that she would "never marry any man on the face of the earth." She kept the letter of her promise, but was married after all to the man of her choice, in this novel Gretna Green. We were fortunate in witnessing a similar scene.

This avenue is about two miles long, and abounds in grotesque curiosities. It ends in Annette's Dome, where a cascade surprises one by bursting from the wall and then disappearing. Lake Purity, near by, is a shallow pool of such transparency that we did not suspect its existence until we walked into it.

Retracing our steps, we soon approach a region of pits and domes. The guide warns us of "danger on the right!" Beside our path yawns a chasm called the Side-saddle Pit, from the shape of a projecting rock, on which we seat ourselves and watch with fearful interest the rolls of oiled paper lighted by the guide and dropped into the abyss. Down they go in a fiery spiral, burning long enough to give us a view of its corrugated sides and of a mass of blackened sticks and timbers a hundred feet below, remnants of a bridge once spanning the chasm.

The Bottomless Pit, a short distance

SCENES IN MAMMOTH CAVE.

beyond, is on a still grander scale, and extending, as it does, entirely across the avenue, was long an effectual bar to further progress. It is now spanned by a substantial bridge, which, for the sake of perfect safety, is renewed every four years. Leaning over the hand-rails, we safely admired the blazing rolls as they whirled to and fro, slowly sinking one hundred and seventy-five feet, lighting up the wrinkles and furrows made by the torrent's flow during untold ages.

Shelby's Dome overhead is but a continuation of the great pit upward, with rich water-carved scroll-work and lavishly decorated panels, and here and there a sharp projection.

Turning abruptly back, we follow the guide up and down narrow stair-ways and through a winding passage, till we find ourselves peering through a window-like aperture into profound darkness, that seems intensified by the monotonous sound of dripping water. Tom bids us remain where we are while he seeks a smaller and higher window beyond, through which he thrusts blue lights and blazing rolls, disclosing indescribable wonders to our gaze. This is Gorin's Dome. The floor far below us, about an acre in area, is covered with water. The perpendicular walls, rising out of sight, are draped with three immense stalagmitic curtains, one above another, whose folds, which seem to be loosely floating, are bordered with fringes rich and heavy. These hangings, dight with figures rare and fantastic, fit for Plutonian halls, were woven in Nature's loom by crystal threads of running water.

MAMMOTH CAVE—"THE FAT MAN'S MISERY."

The domes and pits are in fact identical; the name varying as they are seen from above or below. The surface-funnel, or sink-hole, drains the rain-water into the upper tier of cavern chambers; and this may end its work. But when a mass of pebbles is gathered, the whirling water uses this powerful cutting-engine to pierce by a vertical shaft the successive tiers, or floors, until the water level of the lowest cavern is reached. Should the funnel be in any way obstructed, the stream would of necessity cease to flow, and the dripping lime-water would have time to make a stalagmitic deposit. Plainly, no dome can exceed in height the extreme distance between the drainage-level and the surface; which, by barometrical observation, has, for Mammoth Cave, been fixed at 312 feet. There is little doubt that in some instances this altitude is nearly attained. All greater estimates are but imaginary.

We have now a choice of evils between Bunyan's Way, where one must stoop like a pilgrim burdened, and Buchanan's Way, where one must hold his head to one side, after the traditional habit of that eminent statesman. We choose the latter; and presently, by a circular opening over which hangs a threatening trap-door of rock, we are made acquainted with the famous and original Fat Man's Misery, of which all others are but base imitations. It is a serpentine channel, whose walls, eighteen inches apart, change direction eight times in one hundred and five yards; while the average distance from the sandy pathway to the ledge overhead is but five feet. The rocky sides are beautifully marked with waves and ripples, as if running water had been suddenly petrified. There seems to have been first a horizontal opening between two strata of limestone, by taking advantage of which this singular winding way was chiseled, from whose embrace we gladly emerge into Great Relief, where we can straighten our spines, and enjoy once more the luxury of a full breath.

It was formerly supposed that if this passage were blocked up, escape from the regions beyond would be impossible. But

not long ago the "Corkscrew" was discovered, an intricate web of fissures, by means of which a good climber, after mounting three ladders, crawling through narrow openings, and leaping from rock to rock, ascending thus amid the wildest confusion for one hundred and fifty feet, gains a landing at last, only a thousand yards from the entrance to the cave, and cuts off two or three miles of travel. Visitors generally come in one way and go out the other, and usually regard the route last chosen the worst, whichever it may have been.

Barton was inclined "to draw this 'Corkscrew';" and leaving him to do so, Tom and I entered an avenue aside from the regular routes, and which he himself had not explored for seven years. After much stooping and creeping, we emerged from the low, narrow passage, and found ourselves standing on a terrace thirty feet long and fifteen wide, whence we peered into a realm of empty darkness. Our lamps revealed neither floor, nor roof, nor opposite wall. Tom said that this was Mammoth Dome, sole rival of Gorin's Dome, the grandest halls in all this domain of silence and of night. I directed him to leave me here, and to return at once for my comrade and for fire-works.

THE CORKSCREW.

Not until Tom's glimmering light was gone, and his retreating steps had ceased to echo along the corridor, did I realize my lonely situation. There were some unexpected causes of delay, so that nearly two hours elapsed before they came. I sat on the edge of the terrace for a time, and amused myself by throwing lighted papers down, thus discovering that the floor was less than forty feet below me, and was accessible by a rude ladder blackened with age. Here and there a rung was missing, and I hesitated to trust such a fragile support. Finding the solitude and darkness insupportable, I retreated with my lamp to the avenue by which we had come, and whiled away the time catching cave crickets, till Tom and Barton arrived with twenty lamps and a supply of red fire and bengolas.

Carefully descending the treacherous ladder, we lighted up the huge dome and found the dimensions to be about 400 feet in length, 150 in width, and 250 in height, as nearly as we could estimate without the aid of instruments. The floor, strewn with slippery rocks, slopes down to a pool that receives a water-fall from the summit of the dome. The walls are curtained by alabaster drapery in vertical folds, varying in size from a pipe-stem to a saw-log, and decorated by heavy fringes at intervals of about twenty feet. A huge gate-way, at the farther end of the hall, opens into a room so like the ruins of Luxor and Karnak that we named it the Egyptian Temple. The floor of this apartment is paved with stalagmitic blocks, stained by red and black oxides into a kind of mosaic. Six colossal columns, eighty feet high by twenty-five in diameter, stand in a semicircle flanked by pyramidal towers. The material of the shafts is gray oölite, fluted by deep furrows with sharp ridges between; the capitals are projecting slabs of limestone; the whole column, in each instance, is veneered with yellow stalagmite, rich as jasper, and covered by tracery as elaborate as Chinese carving; and the bases are garnished by mushroom-shaped stalagmites. The largest of these is Caliban's Cushion. While examining this, I noticed an opening behind the third column in the row, and clambering down a steep descent we reached gloomy catacombs underneath; but returned without fully exploring them, on account of the extreme difficulty of progress.

One day we learned that a large party from Nashville were to visit River Hall and the regions beyond the subterranean streams; and, as they would first make a detour by the pits, we easily got the start of them by climbing down the Corkscrew. On entering River Hall, we found our path skirting the edge of cliffs 60 feet high and 100 feet long, embracing the sullen waters of what is called the Dead Sea. Descending a flight of steps, we came to a cascade, but a little farther on, said to be a re-appearance of the water-fall at the entrance, suggesting the idea that the cave has doubled on its track.

Our speculations on this mystery were broken in upon by the hilarious sounds heralding the party under Matt's escort, long before they came in view. There never was a prettier sight than this merry company, sixty in all, as with flashing lamps and spangled costumes they skirted the somber terrace, astonishing the steeps of that gloomy sea by the loud refrain of "Litoria" and other jolly college songs. They wound past us, in single file, disappearing behind a rocky mass to come into view again on the natural bridge, whence they swung their lamps to catch sight of the River Styx.

This body of water is said to be over 400 feet long and 40 feet wide. Our attempts at fathoming its depth resulted in one of us falling in, and from his appearance on crawl-

MAMMOTH CAVE — IN "THE DEVIL'S ARM-CHAIR"

ing out, we judged that he found an abundance of mud under an uncertain amount of water.

Lake Lethe comes next—a broad sheet of water formerly crossed by boats, but now skirted by a narrow path at the foot of steep walls ninety feet above the oblivious wave, and leading to a pontoon at the neck of the lake, from which we step upon a beach of the finest yellow sand, extending to Echo River, a distance of 500 yards, under a lofty ceiling mottled with white and black limestones, like snow-clouds drifting in a wintry sky. A rise of five feet would cover this sandy walk, which is its condition for from four to eight months in every year. Fortunately the streams were low at the time of our visit, as they usually are in summer.

The connection of the cave rivers with Green River has been proved by the simple experiment of throwing a quantity of chaff upon them, which comes to the surface in the upper and lower big springs; deep, bubbling pools, lying half a mile apart, under the cliffs bristling with hemlocks and pines. When these pools are submerged by a freshet in Green River, the streams in the cave are united into a continuous body of water. At rare intervals the rise is so high as to touch the iron railing sixty feet above the Dead Sea; and for some reason the subsidence within is less rapid than that without. In order to save from destruction, at such times, the uncouth little fleet, built of planks and timber, every one of which was brought in through passes we had traversed with difficulty empty-handed, the boats are securely fastened, when not in use, by long ropes of twisted grape-vines that let them swim with the flood.

Four of these boats now await us on the banks of Echo River. Each has seats on the gunwales for twenty passengers, while the guide stands in the bow and propels the primitive craft by a long paddle, or by grasping projecting rocks. The river's width varies from twenty to two hundred feet, and its length is about three-quarters of a mile.

The low arch soon rises to a height varying from ten to thirty feet, while the plummet

THE DEAD SEA.

ENTRANCE OF PURGATORY AND ECHO RIVER.

shows a still greater depth below. The river cannot properly be said to have any shore, for throughout its entire extent there are only one or two points where a foothold could be gained. Hence, the guides exercise the strictest authority, in order to guard against accidents.

Tom secures for our exclusive use a boat smaller than those into which the others crowd. He then draws from a hiding-place a hand-net, and tries to catch for us a few of the famous eyeless fish, that dart to and fro, but vanish on the least agitation of the water. His success at this time was not very encouraging. But subsequently, on other trips, we captured numerous specimens, from two to six inches in length, and usually destitute of even rudimentary organs of vision. Several, however, had protuberances, or sightless eyes, and one had good eye-sight. The gradations of color are from olive-brown to pure white, while some are perfectly colorless and transparent. They are said to be viviparous; and, instead of bones, have mere cartilage. Agassiz held that these cave-fish "were created under the circumstances in which they now live, within the limits over which they range, and with the structural peculiarities which characterize them at the present day." But it is doubtful if there is more variability than can be explained by simple retardation through successive generations.

Along the water's edge are cavities, varying in size from a few inches to many feet, washed out by the stream. The Nashville wag saw his opportunity to break the silence that had settled over the voyagers, and shouted with absurd glee, pointing to the cavities:

"Oh, see these little bits o' caves—three for five cents!"

The solemn echoes caught his silly tones, and bore them, as if in derision, hither and thither and far away. When the peals of laughter that followed had died away, a quiet lady in black velvet led us in sacred song. The concord of sweet sounds was surprisingly agreeable; but the tones followed each other too rapidly to secure full justice.

Allowing the Nashville party to go on without us, I passed the rest of the day on Echo River, alone with Tom, floating over its strangely transparent water, as if gliding through the air, and trying every echo its arches were capable of producing. A single aërial vibration given with energy, as by a pistol-shot, rebounded from rock to rock. The din awakened by discordant sounds was frightful. On the other hand, when the voice gave the tones of a full chord *seriatim*, they came back in a sweeping *arpeggio.* Flute-music produced charming reverberations. The finest vocal effect followed the utterance, as strongly and firmly as possible, of the key-note of that long vault, letting all other sounds meanwhile cease; the wonderful vibrations thus caused were prolonged for from fifteen to thirty seconds after the original tone had been delivered.

An extraordinary result was obtained by the guide's agitating the water vigorously with his broad paddle, and then seating himself in silence by my side. The first sound that broke the stillness was like the tinkling of silver bells. Larger and heavier bells then seemed to take up the strange melody, as the waves sought out the cavities in the rock. And then it appeared as if all chimes of all cathedrals had conspired to raise a tempest of sweet sounds. They then died away to utter silence. We still sat in expectation. Lo, as if from some deep recess that had been hitherto forgotten, came a tone tender and profound; after which, like gentle memories, were re-awakened all the mellow sounds that had gone before, until River Hall rang again. This concert was prolonged for several minutes, until the agitation of the waters had wholly subsided. Those who try their own voices are pleased to have the hollow wall faithfully give back every shout and song, whimsical cry or merry peal; but the nymphs of Echo River reserve their choicest harmonies for those who are willing in silence to listen to the voice of many waters.

CROGHAN HALL AND MAELSTROM.

A SNOW CLOUD, MAMMOTH CAVE.

Roaring River and Mystic River are considerable streams; but, lying on side avenues, they are seldom visited, and may now be passed with mere mention.

All these lakes and rivers are liable to overflow, as has already been remarked, completely filling this part of the cave. These remote regions are never entered when there are signs of a flood. Large cans of oil are, however, stored securely, against the contingency of a party's being shut in by rising waters; so that the lamps may be kept burning. Moreover, a discovery has been made, within a year, of a passage leading out beyond the rivers by a circuit of ten miles. It contains numerous objects of interest, but is so rugged and contracted in places as to deter visitors from attempting to go through, except in case of necessity.

Continuing our journey by way of Silliman's Avenue and El Ghor, picturesque passes where many fantastic objects are pointed out, we arrive at Hebe's Spring. Here, by climbing a ladder and crawling through a hole in the roof, we are admitted to an upper tier of caverns. Tom ignites blue fire, and we are surprised to find ourselves in a vineyard! Countless nodules and globules simulate clusters on clusters of luscious grapes, burdening hundreds of boughs, and gleaming with party-colored tints through the dripping dew.

Washington Hall is but a smoke-stained lunch-room. The ceiling of a room near by is dotted with semi-spherical masses of snowy gypsum, each of which is from two to ten inches in diameter, looking like a snowball hurled against the wall and sticking there. Snow-ball Room is a fitting vestibule to the treasure house of alabaster brilliants beyond it, where we tarry long with ever-increasing delight.

What words can picture forth the beauty of Cleveland's Cabinet? Wyandot and other caverns may have galleries like it in kind, but none to be compared with it either in extent or symmetry. We loiter beneath spotless arches of fifty feet span, where the fancy is at once enlivened and bewildered by a mimicry of every flower that grows in the garden, forest or prairie, from the modest daisy to the flaunting helianthus.

Select for examination a single one of these enchanting blossoms, the "oulopholites" of the mineralogist. Consider the charms of this queenly rose that has unfolded its petals in Mary's Bower. From a central stem gracefully curl countless crystals fibrous and pellucid; each tiny crystal is in itself a study; each fascicle of curved prisms is wonderful; and the whole creation is a miracle of beauty.

Now imagine this mimic flower multiplied from one to a hundred, a thousand, a myriad! Move down the dazzling vista, as if in a dream of Elysium,—not for a few yards, or rods, but for *two miles*. All is virgin white, except here and there a little patch of gray limestone, or a spot bronzed by some metallic stain, or, again, as we purposely vary the lovely monotony by burning colored lights. Midway is a great cross overhead, formed by the natural

EGYPTIAN TEMPLE, MAMMOTH CAVE.

A Stalactite.

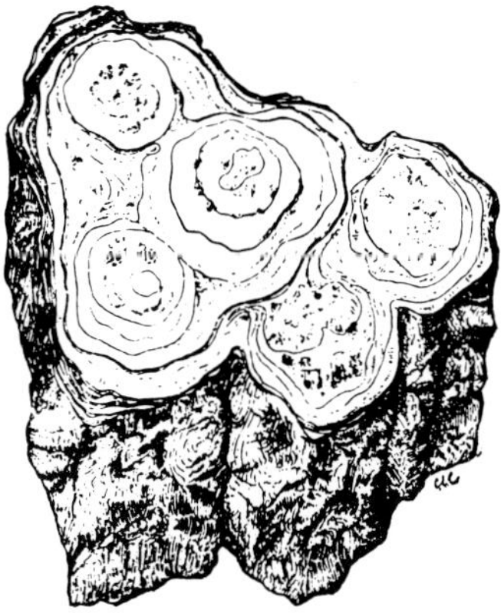

Cross-section of Stalactite. (Produced by several separate stalactites growing together.)

grouping of stone rosettes. Floral clusters, bouquets, wreaths, garlands, embellish nearly every foot of the ceiling and walls; while the very soil sparkles with trodden jewels. The pendulous fringes of the night-blooming cereus are rivaled by the snowy plumes that float from rifts and crevices, forever safe from the withering glare of daylight. Clumps of lilies, pale pansies, blanched tulips, drooping fuchsias, sprays of asters, spikes of tuberoses, wax-leaved magnolias,—but why exhaust the botanical catalogue? The fancy finds every gem of the green-house and parterre in this crystalline conservatory. Earlier visitors (Professor Locke in 1842, and Bayard Taylor in 1855) describe long sprays, like stalks of celery, running vines, and branches of a chandelier; but it has been impossible to guard such exquisite formations from covetous fingers. Happily the subtle forces of nature are still at work, slowly replacing by fresh productions what has gone to the mineralogist's cabinet or the amateur's *etagere*.

Stalactite Formation in Limestone. (The arrows show the direction of the movement of the water.)

The most ardent admirer of Mammoth Cave must admit its poverty in stalactitic adornments; especially when compared with the wonderful cave at Luray, in Virginia, which, though not exceeding fifty acres in area, has millions of stalactites, reflected from hundreds of crystal pools. But, on the other hand, Luray has no gypsum rosettes, and its largest lake is only fifty feet in diameter. This remarkable difference is due to the fact that while Mammoth Cave is excavated from an immense mass of homogeneous limestone, affording few opportunities for the formation of drip-stone, the cave of Luray is cut from rock broken up into countless rifts and seams by the upheaval of the Appalachian range. Hence, the two are as unlike as the Mississippi River and Lake George, or as Niagara Falls and Watkins Glen.

THE STYX, MAMMOTH CAVE.

Beyond a rocky hill and a dismal gorge lies Croghan's Hall, and a pit called the Maelstrom, which ends the cave so far as it has been explored in this direction. It is due to the memory of a daring youth to tell how Mr. W. C. Prentice, son of the poet and editor, George D. Prentice, descended this abyss in quest of adventures.

As the guides tell the story, they furnished a rope, down which the young hero descended undaunted, amid fearful and enchanting scenes, then first lighted since creation's morning by the feeble rays of his solitary lamp. Midway he encountered a water-fall, spouting from the rocky wall, into whose sparkling shower he unavoidably swung. Escaping all dangers, he stood at last on the solid rock, 190 feet below his comrades, who now found that it taxed their utmost strength to lift him and the amount of cable that had been paid out. On his way up, Prentice swung himself into a huge niche for the purpose of exploration, whence he roamed through wide and wondrous chambers till checked by rocky barriers. Then, returning to the place where he had fastened his rope to a stalactite, he found it disengaged and dangling beyond his reach. Ingeniously twisting the wires of his lamp into a long hook, he caught hold again, and signaled to the guides to draw him up. It is said (and one is expected to believe) that they did this with such zeal that the cable was fired by friction, and that one of the guides crawled out on the beam and emptied a flask of water on the burning rope. The whole story, with all its embellishments, is done into spirited verse by Rev. George Lansing Taylor. The hero himself, whose life was so miraculously spared, finally sacrificed it, in 1860, for the lost cause.

A charming excursion was from Washington Hall down Marion Avenue to the Crystal Paradise. Another was from the Vineyard, as a starting point, and through a long winding arcade to Lucy's Dome, rarely visited because somewhat difficult of access. This is the loftiest cave-dome yet discovered anywhere in the world, and in some of its features it is unlike any we had seen before. By burning three Bengal lights and a quantity of magnesium, simultaneously, we barely caught sight of the oval apex, more than 300 feet overhead. A twin dome rises by its side, and a tall Gothic archway connects the two, at a point 150 feet above the floor.

It was only after gaining considerable experience in cave-hunting that we ventured in alone; even then keeping to well-

THE BOTTOMLESS PIT, MAMMOTH CAVE.

beaten paths, and noting landmarks with care; or, if tempted to explore new ground, indicating the way out by repeatedly marking arrows on the wall. The penalty of losing one's way amid these awful solitudes is a painful bewilderment, often amounting to temporary mental derangement. Hence, as a rule, the services of a guide cannot safely be dispensed with, and guests should respect his authority; for the law holds him responsible for the safe return of those put under his care. Persons accidentally separated from their party should quietly stay in one place till deliverance comes.

We witnessed, one day, a narrow escape on the part of an excitable gentleman, who trusted to his own guidance. His companions were following their guide up the chimney-like corkscrew, and he caught at the bright idea of getting ahead of them by the longer route. He started off alone and on the full run. We followed him, more out of curiosity than from apprehension. His lamp went out; but in his eagerness he did not stop to relight it, relying on the scattered rays of ours behind him. Suddenly Tom darted forward and grasped the stranger in his strong arms. We abruptly halted. There, within a single step, yawned the Side-saddle Pit, on whose black rocks, a hundred feet below, the man would have fallen, had it not been for Tom's presence of mind.

The full moon was riding in a cloudless sky, when we emerged from our last day's journey in the great cavern. We had, as usual, a practical proof of the purity of the exhilarating cave atmosphere, by its contrast with that of the outer world, which seemed heavy and suffocating. The odors of trees, grass, weeds and flowers were strangely intensified and overpowering. The result of a too sudden transition is frequently faintness, headache and vertigo. Hence the pleasant custom of lingering awhile on the threshold, where the outer and inner airs mingle. Resting thus, on rustic seats near the entrance, we interchanged our views.

On the whole, Mammoth Cave greatly exceeded, though differing from, our expectations. Yet there was a want of full satisfaction. It was gratifying to be assured by Tom that we had probably tramped to and fro, in and out, about one hundred miles; but how did he know?

The time will come when much more will be known of Mammoth Cave than is possible under existing restrictions. There ought to be a better understanding between the owners and the public. There should be increased facilities of access, along with a sufficient guarantee against any infringement of proprietary rights; then let surveyors measure, geologists hammer, and archæologists delve, till the secrets of this subterranean realm are unearthed, and instead of mysteries, conjectures and estimates, we have definite knowledge. We were grateful, however, for impressions received and memories retained of wonderful scenes and strange adventures. Feelings akin to friendship had sprung up within us for Mammoth Cave; and it was with positive regret that we finally turned away from the fern-fringed chasm, lying there in the soft moonlight, where the sparkling cascade throws pearly drops from the mossy ridge, and spreads its mist like a silver veil.

THE END.

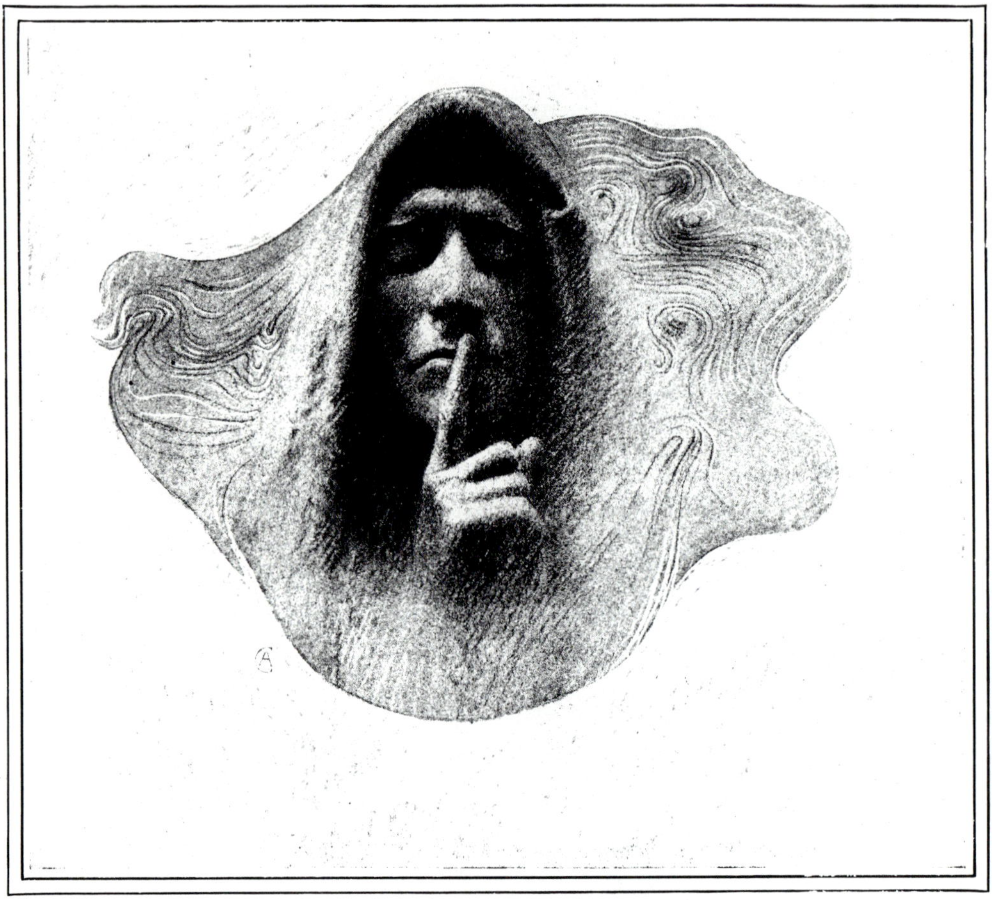

«THE SPIRIT OF ETERNAL, CHANGELESS SILENCE REIGNS SUPREME.»

We are told that this is the end of the cave; but it is only one of the many ends, and some of the avenues have been closed by fallen rocks or by the stalactite growth, and the real end is yet unknown. We retrace our steps, and after a wandering of nine hours emerge from the cave into the oppressive air of the upper world. We have seen nothing more beautiful than the rosy light of the setting sun as we look out from the dark chasm. We turn for a last lingering look into the wonderful, mysterious under-world, where the spirit of eternal, changeless Silence reigns supreme.

—John R. Proctor
formerly State Geologist of Kentucky
in *Century Magazine,* 1898, p. 658